# JESUS, COMPANION in My SUFFERING

"We all suffer, and we are all called at times to minister to others who are suffering. Reading and sharing these reflections will help us reflect on our own suffering and also to bring the love of Christ into the lives of people who are suffering."

**Deacon Ed Shoener**
Compiler and editor of *When a Loved One Dies by Suicide*

"Joyce Rupp is a soul midwife, guiding us with a gentle but strong hand as we struggle to birth something new from the depths of ourselves. Our griefs, large and small, are safe here; we can trust they will be tended with care. *Jesus, Companion in My Suffering* is the Lent book we have long needed."

**Shannon K. Evans**
Author of *Rewilding Motherhood*

"Visiting the heart of Joyce Rupp remains a pleasure. She owns her limitations, which make mine feel less lonely, and her God-names are inventive: 'Surprising Healer,' 'Unexpected Visitor,' 'Keen Listener.' The quick daily plunge of spiritual direction in this book is bracing. Disappointment, failure, and being out of control are never taboo."

**Alice Camille**
Author of *Working Toward Sainthood: Daily Reflections for Lent*

REFLECTIONS *for the* LENTEN JOURNEY

# JESUS, COMPANION *in My* SUFFERING

## JOYCE RUPP

AVE MARIA PRESS AVE Notre Dame, Indiana

Founded in 1865, Ave Maria Press is a ministry of the United States Province of Holy Cross.

www.avemariapress.com

Paperback: ISBN-13 978-1-64680-192-3

E-book: ISBN-13 978-1-64680-193-0

Cover image © gettyimages.com.

Cover and text design by Brian C. Conley.

Printed and bound in the United States of America.

*Library of Congress Cataloging-in-Publication Data is available.*

# CONTENTS

Introduction ........................................................... ix

*Ash Wednesday to First Sunday of Lent*

Ash Wednesday: Healing for Everyone .............. 2

Thursday: Willing to Approach Suffering .......... 4

Friday: Preventable Complaints ........................... 6

Saturday: Disappointments ................................... 8

*First Week of Lent*

Sunday: Tempted Away from Good .................. 12

Monday: At the Mercy of Another ..................... 14

Tuesday: Poverty .................................................. 16

Wednesday: Anxiety and Worry ........................ 18

Thursday: Judging Others ................................... 20

Friday: Trusting the Healing Process ................ 22

Saturday: Failure .................................................. 24

*Second Week of Lent*

    Sunday: Grief .......................................................... 28

    Monday: Dismissing Those Who Suffer ........... 30

    Tuesday: Out of Control ..................................... 32

    Wednesday: Fear ................................................. 34

    Thursday: Less Than We Hoped to Be ............. 36

    Friday: Compassion Fatigue ............................... 38

    Saturday: Embarrassment ................................... 40

*Third Week of Lent*

    Sunday: Loneliness ............................................. 44

    Monday: Helpful, Healing Hands ..................... 46

    Tuesday: Weeping for What Is to Come ........... 48

    Wednesday: Depression ...................................... 50

    Thursday: Hypocrisy ........................................... 52

    Friday: Moved with Compassion ...................... 54

    Saturday: Poor Self-Image ................................. 56

*Fourth Week of Lent*

    Sunday: Admitting Wrongdoing ....................... 60

    Monday: Rejection ............................................. 62

    Tuesday: Exasperation ........................................ 64

Wednesday: A Healing Touch ........................... 66

Thursday: Burdened ...................................... 68

Friday: Finding Fault ..................................... 70

Saturday: Ending Relationships ...................... 72

Fifth Week of Lent

Sunday: Accepting the Dying Process ............. 76

Monday: Carrying the Cross ........................... 78

Tuesday: Betrayal .......................................... 80

Wednesday: Comforting Caregivers ................ 82

Thursday: Our Own Worst Enemy .................. 84

Friday: Shame ............................................... 86

Saturday: Recognizing the Truth .................... 88

Sixth Week of Lent (Holy Week)

Passion (Palm) Sunday: Unfinished Work ....... 92

Monday: Violence .......................................... 94

Tuesday: Standing by the Cross ...................... 96

Wednesday: Powerless .................................... 98

Holy Thursday: The Hour of Anguish ............ 100

Good Friday: Feeling Abandoned ................... 102

Holy Saturday: Giving Our Life for Another . 104

Easter Sunday: Joy beyond Suffering .............. 106

Questions for Reflection ..................................... 109
Notes ....................................................................111

# INTRODUCTION

> You will have pain, but your pain will turn into joy. When a woman is in labor, she has pain, because her hour has come. But when her child is born, she no longer remembers the anguish because of the joy of having brought a human being into the world.
>
> —John 16:20–21

In Lucy Hone's inspiring TED Talk on grief and resiliency, she begins by asking her audience to stand if they have experienced the adversities she is about to name. Eventually, almost all of the large group are standing. "Look around," Professor Hone suggests, "see that you are not alone."[1]

Although unwanted, suffering exists as one of humanity's commonalities. Whether this harsh intruder derives from personal experience or from a global perspective, everyone knows what it is like to hurt. Childhood disappointments, adolescent struggles with self-image, adult heartaches, pandemics, hostile political divisions, and dangerous climate change—there's little doubt that suffering finds its way to us.

Not only do we benefit from the strength of our kinship with other humans who know loss, illness, and defeat, but also we have a guide at the heart of Christianity to assist us in being with those pains. In Jesus, we find insight and inspiration to encounter our struggles, along with the assurance of being able to move through and beyond those heartaches.

Sometimes it is best to step aside from suffering to protect our mental and emotional health, but usually when we disregard what upsets the mind and heart, it just digs in more deeply. Teachers of spirituality and psychology tell us that this resistance leads to more, rather than less, discomfort. Unattended hurts fester and work against joy and satisfaction. While suffering in itself has no transformational value and is certainly not to be sought for its own sake, our soreness of spirit can awaken dormant goodness in us. Much depends on how we approach and tend to our misfortunes.

Understandably, we would want to run from what ails us. One Lent I was scheduled to lead a weekend retreat for a congregation. When I suggested to the pastor that the focus be the life-death-resurrection cycle of Jesus, he balked: "Oh, we don't do Lent here, just Easter." I changed the title to appease him but went ahead and spoke about how life consists of a continuous cycle that includes moving through "death or letting go" before hope arrives. This "death" includes anything in life that rips away gladness, leaving us feeling empty, wandering, or overcome. As it turned out, the retreatants were fully engaged, welcomed deeper meaning for their lives, and expressed gratitude for restored confidence in meeting the daily challenges confronting them.

I learned the value of facing suffering, whether the suffering is inherent in daily challenges or is something more devastating, such as the experience of my twenty-three-year–old brother drowning. For fifteen years I managed to sidestep this loss even though a nagging sorrow regularly leeched my joy. Finally, I went on a thirty-day Ignatian retreat with the specific intention of coming to terms with that death. During those four weeks, my retreat leader directed me to meditate on specific gospel passages. I spent a lot of time looking at how Jesus approached his own and others' adversities. As I pondered how his empathic love threads through the gospel narratives, I came to know Jesus as my mentor of compassion.

During that retreat, I finally understood the experience of my brother's death as being part of the human condition and that suffering can enable me to grow in being more like this mentor of love. Coming to terms with my sorrow also moved me to discover my inherent empathy for those who hurt. But that was not all that came from the retreat. I also gained reassurance about the humanity of Jesus, someone who would understand and relate to what I go through because he experienced these things in his own unique way. He felt sorrow, anguish, and physical pain; he knew what it was like for his beliefs to be questioned and rejected. He got angry, irritated, and disappointed. He lived among people who suffered from all sorts of physical conditions. He listened to family squabbles and expressed his distress at the lack of societal justice. All of this assures me that I can make it through the difficulties that come my way. I can learn from Jesus, drawing both courage and comfort in doing so.

Another help I've gained from the life and teachings of Jesus includes understanding the necessity of lament. He allowed himself to feel his pain, whether grieving over the death of a friend or feeling abandoned when he hung on the Cross. When his disciples told hurting ones crying out to shut up, Jesus deliberately drew near them instead. Author Marilyn McEntyre suggests making a litany of our laments:

> To look at the whole, sorry lot of our sufferings can be an important step toward release. . . . Those of us who were taught not to complain, to keep a stiff upper lip, to take a certain pride in what we can put up with—we may need to list our laments more than others. To give ourselves that permission may liberate the energy we expend on keeping a lid on what needs to be released, or at least seen clearly enough to enable us to devise effective ways of living with what we cannot entirely dispel.[2]

We each have our laments, and from them, we can make our litany. As you pray with the reflections in *Jesus, Companion in My Sufferings*, you'll find some aspect of his own experience of suffering or that of other persons who bear some form of hurt in that litany. On occasion his teaching related to suffering will be the focus. I hope these reflections stir and expand your compassion for self and others.

We become more compassionate and kindhearted when we acknowledge and care for our broken-open hearts because we sense our solidarity with other persons' sufferings. Joseph Bernardin, the empathetic Roman Catholic cardinal from Chicago, affirmed this after being unjustly accused of perpetrating sexual abuse and later being diagnosed with terminal cancer:

> As Christians, if we are to love as Jesus loved, we must first come to terms with suffering. Like Jesus, we simply cannot be cool and detached from our fellow human beings. Our years of living as Christians will be years of suffering for and with other people. Like Jesus, we will love others only if we walk with them in the valley of darkness—the dark valley of sickness, the dark valley of moral dilemmas, the dark valley of oppressive structures and diminished rights.[3]

May this profound wisdom accompany your journey through Lent.

(Suggestions for individual or group integration of each week's reflections are located on page 109.)

# Ash Wednesday to First Sunday of Lent

# HEALING FOR EVERYONE

> As the sun was setting, all those who had any
> who were sick with various kinds of diseases
> brought them to him; and he laid his hands on
> each of them and cured them.
>
> —Luke 4:40

Throughout the gospels, people arrive with a variety of sufferings for Jesus to heal. No type of ailment or hurt is too little, too large, or too strange for him to tend. He encounters everyone personally—touching them, placing his hands upon them, flesh to flesh, and coming close to the ill, soul to soul. And he does so for *each* of them. He treats them not as impersonal objects but rather as people who matter, people not only in need of his attentiveness but also worthy of it. Did Jesus fear catching a disease? Did he flinch when he saw festering wounds or smelled the stench of the unbathed? Did he feel repelled by the harsh manifestation of an emotional or mental illness? Whatever stirred within Jesus, those emotions did not hinder his attitude and ability to alleviate people's ill health and bring about greater wellness for those who sought it.

This Lent we attend to whatever produces suffering for us, whether this be our own incompleteness regarding spiritual growth or hurts resulting from physical, emotional, mental, relational, or social issues. There is no illness or personal struggle that cannot be brought to the One Who Heals. Let us approach with confidence and humble trust, asking to be touched by this transforming love.

---

Companion in My Suffering,
as I step into another Lenten season,
I bring to you what requires your graced touch.
You know what will further my well-being.
I open my mind and heart to you with confidence
that you will tend with care what troubles me.

*Today*: I reflect on the part of my life containing
        discontent.

# WILLING TO APPROACH SUFFERING

A leper came to him begging him, and kneeling he said to him, "If you choose, you can make me clean." Moved with pity, Jesus stretched out his hand and touched him, and said to him, "I do choose. Be made clean!" Immediately the leprosy left him, and he was made clean.

—Mark 1:40–42

Think of it—Jesus *chose* to reach out his hand and touch a man covered with infectious sores. He deliberately stepped closer to suffering. Not only was this viewed with abhorrence by his society, but also it meant that his planned day was interrupted. Yet Jesus stopped. He paid attention. He reached out. He touched the untouchable. In doing so, a man's life was changed forever.

The hand of Jesus reaching out to the leper serves as an image of our relationship with suffering. One way to enter Lent and give ourselves to further transformation is by identifying what hurts in us, listening kindly to what troubles us and won't let us alone. What issues of body, mind, or spirit keep nagging for our compassionate attention? Much growth can occur through a willingness to lean toward what we'd rather avoid, to tend what rubs against our will and chafes our heart. This might be touching on our personal unfinishedness in a way that avoids beating ourselves up or facing externally difficult situations with care. It might be reaching out to a hurting friend or neighbor or going far beyond that to the many who suffer across our planet.

---

Channel of Healing,
today I join with you in being willing
to tend to my own suffering and that of others.
Loosen my grip on avoiding what I dread.
Free me to approach it with a heart of compassion.
I place my trust in you.

*Today*: I reach out to a person who is hurting.

# PREVENTABLE COMPLAINTS

> A woman named Martha welcomed him into her home. She had a sister named Mary, who sat at the Lord's feet and listened to what he was saying. But Martha was distracted by her many tasks; so she came to him and asked, "Lord, do you not care that my sister has left me to do all the work by myself? Tell her then to help me." But the Lord answered her, "Martha, Martha, you are worried and distracted by many things; there is need of only one thing. Mary has chosen the better part."
>
> —Luke 10:38–42

There's Martha in the kitchen, getting more upset with each stirring of the pot. Angry resentment seethes as she goes about what she's doing. When she complains to Jesus, he doesn't support or reassure her. He apparently does not give a hoot about Martha's irritation, perhaps because she's brought her anger upon herself. She extended a welcome to him. But instead of seeing her work as cordial hospitality, she's fuming about having to do it all alone. Martha had a right to ask for Mary's help, but did her whining change things? Better to talk with Mary later about the next time they have visitors and how they could divide the tasks rather than trying to make herself sound like a martyr to them.

I, too, make choices resulting in my being overwhelmed or distressed. Then I complain about it and expect divine intervention to get me out of the mess. Let's ask ourselves, *When this situation next happens, how might I change my attitude or humbly ask for help to ease the tension inside of me?*

---

Abiding Presence,
I invite you to be attentive to me in prayer,
but I resist setting aside my plans and schedule
in order to prepare my distracted heart for this.
If I desire you to abide in the home of my heart,
then I will accept the effort it takes to welcome you.

*Today*: I pay attention to what I gripe about either
silently or aloud.

# DISAPPOINTMENTS

Then he began to reproach the cities in which
most of his deeds of power had been done, because they did not repent. "Woe to you, Chora-
zin! Woe to you, Bethsaida! For if the deeds of
power done in you had been done in Tyre and
Sidon, they would have repented long ago in
sackcloth and ashes."

—Matthew 11:20–21

Jesus certainly sounds disappointed. Despite giving himself fully, the people resisted changing their ways. Like
Jesus, frustration erupts when we weary ourselves by
devoting significant effort to personal or societal causes that ends up having little effect. I felt this way after
hours of preparing talks and traveling a half day to lead
a weekend retreat. I presumed the participants would be
engaged. Instead, they were noticeably distracted. When
I stood before them to speak, they responded as if I were

not there—just kept yakking to one another and scrolling on their phones.

People invariably disappoint us by such things as not understanding our heartache, failing to appreciate a paid-for college education, ignoring our request for assistance, yawning through a homily, not thanking us after the hours we spent preparing a meal, or tearing apart a carefully created vision statement. When disappointment shows up in your life, how do you respond? Mark Nepo suggests in *The Book of Soul* that "there is always another direction on the other side of pain and disappointment, if we can take a breath and look around."[1]

---

Vision for My Spirit,
light the path to restored peace of mind
when I fall on the road of disappointments.
Remind me that you also experienced
your own frustration and discouragement.
Lead me beyond my scratchy emotions.

*Today*: I consider my disappointments and what
I've learned from them.

# First Week of Lent

# TEMPTED AWAY FROM GOOD

> And the Spirit immediately drove [Jesus] out
> into the wilderness. He was in the wilderness
> forty days, tempted by Satan; and he was with
> the wild beasts; and the angels waited on him.
> —Mark 1:12–13

Who of us has not been tempted away from good, having to choose between what would profit our best or worst self? Some deceitful persuasions are sneaky and unsuspecting, while others fly in our face and smack us into immediate attention. Certain people suffer immensely from an illness known as scrupulosity; they are pummeled daily by self-doubt regarding the choices they make in trying to live a virtuous life. For most of us, the experience of temptation is not that intense, but it still requires a decision to go toward what reflects Jesus's teachings instead of giving in to false beguilement.

In the wilderness of the COVID-19 pandemic, I developed an attitude of seeing every unmasked person I met as my enemy. I'd come home filled with rancor that depleted my positive energy. It weakened my ability to write anything inspiring and left my spirit soured. Only when the inner hostility fanned into a flame did I recognize it as the temptation it was: *to stop loving my neighbor as myself.* I learned the importance of being attentive to my thoughts, my emotions and their sources, and how quickly I can blame others by ignoring what needs to change within myself. I still did not agree with unmasked strangers, but I no longer condemned them as ruthless adversaries.

---

Inner Strength,
I draw much hope and encouragement
from knowing you, too, were beguiled
and taunted to abandon your truest self.
With your grace, I can make good choices
and not succumb to false satisfactions.

*Today*: I name what tempts me away from good.

# AT THE MERCY OF ANOTHER

> One man was there who had been ill for thirty-eight years. When Jesus saw him lying there and knew that he had been there a long time, he said to him, "Do you want to be made well?" The sick man answered him, "Sir, I have no one to put me into the pool when the water is stirred up; and while I am making my way, someone else steps down ahead of me."
>
> —John 5:5–7

Imagine thirty-eight years of illness, being physically disabled, struggling to be healed, but never attaining it. The restorative pool in this story revives my memory of the fresh spring flowing in Lourdes, France. At that site, the ill and infirm, unable to reach the healing water by themselves, are brought to the water by compassionate volunteers—strangers in whom they place their trust. The daily, long procession of these helpers pushing gurneys and wheelchairs is a heart-touching scene.

When we search for a pool of healing to make it through a difficulty—whether the pool is a literal one, such as the one at Lourdes, or a figurative one—this requires a vulnerable willingness to admit we can't do everything on our own—no matter how self-reliant we attempt to be. This is especially true of inner suffering. When we yearn for another to forgive us, we ask and wait for their response. When unresolved grief or past childhood trauma assails us, we place ourselves in the care of a counselor to assist us in our recovery. When we lose the way on our spiritual path, we turn to a pastor or spiritual companion for guidance.

---

Merciful Heart,
you teach me by your constant kindness
to be there for those who need assistance.
Your response also assures me that I, too,
must set aside my independent self at times
and humbly ask for what will aid my healing.

*Today*: I deliberately ask someone to pray for my
well-being.

# POVERTY

There was a rich man who was dressed in purple and fine linen and who feasted sumptuously every day. And at his gate lay a poor man named Lazarus, covered with sores, who longed to satisfy his hunger with what fell from the rich man's table. . . . The poor man died and was carried away by the angels to be with Abraham. The rich man also died and was buried. In Hades, where he was being tormented, he looked up and saw Abraham far away with Lazarus by his side.

—Luke 16:19–23

This parable demonstrates the great divide between the "haves" and "have nots." Its message implies dire consequences for cold-hearted persons such as the rich man in the story, who refuses to share from his extravagance. This parable echoes in attitudes and voices today that ignore the plight of individuals and groups whose pleas to move beyond destitution and the injustice of lopsided prosperity go unheard or denied. I, too, am a modern "rich man" when I look at my own bounteous life and what I share in comparison to all I have. With easy access to medical care, food, and essential literacy, I'm among the small percentage of humans able to benefit from these riches.

I doubt Jesus meant this parable to "scare the hell" out of his listeners by instilling fear of eternal damnation. Given his compassionate spirit, he sought to have them become aware of any hard-heartedness they held toward the "have nots" while urging them to assist in providing for the people deprived of life's necessities.

---

Justice Seeker,
I desire to walk in your compassionate footsteps,
to not vacillate in contributing what I possess
to the many who are lacking life's essentials.
Turn my heart away from callous indifference;
steer me toward people who live in poverty.

*Today*: I give away something of value to people
who have less than I do.

# ANXIETY AND WORRY

Do not let your hearts be troubled. Believe in God, believe also in me. . . . And if I go and prepare a place for you, I will come again and will take you to myself, so that where I am, there you may be also.

—John 14:1, 3

It's nigh impossible to keep every tiny bit of worry away from us. We might be steeped in equanimity but still find ourselves fraught with unwanted concerns that steal our peacefulness. Both little and big things can disturb our equilibrium—maybe a costly automobile problem; a serious, unexplained infection; or something as simple as concern about preparing dinner for unexpected guests or having to stand before a group to read the minutes of a meeting.

Jesus told his disciples to not be troubled even though his death neared. He wanted to prepare them for the heartache ahead and to assure them that something beyond that sadness would restore their peacefulness. He promised to be with them in a new way. Similarly, when we enter situations that produce anxiety, we can trust there is more than what we presently experience. Beneath what troubles us lies a durable resilience and a graced strength at the core of our being. When worry tries to carve its way inside, we turn in confidence to the encouraging message of Jesus to not let our hearts be troubled or be afraid. With divine assistance, we *will* make it through disturbing times and recover our inner harmony, just as the disciples did.

---

Source of Equanimity,
when anxiety and worry tumble around
inside my apprehensive interior realm,
I will turn to you with confidence,
knowing you understand my difficulties
and that you desire to provide peace for my life.

*Today*: I take what I worry about to the One who
promises peace.

# JUDGING OTHERS

Do not judge, so that you may not be judged. . . .
Why do you see the speck in your neighbor's eye,
but do not see the log in your own eye?

—Matthew 7:1, 3

Of course, it is nigh impossible to get a log into our eye, but what Jesus emphasizes here with hyperbole and metaphor is that we ought to pull our focus away from what's wrong with other people. We have plenty of our own stuff to take care of and amend in order to be our true self. Despite this reality, I still find it challenging to withdraw my mental comments about everyone else. My brain insists on comparing what I believe and value, how I decide to live and act, to that of both familiar persons and strangers.

I think about this when I look out the windows at my place of prayer. I enjoy seeing the beauty of each season through them, but summer rains and winter snows create many smudges that prevent me from fully enjoying the view. One smudge is not a problem, but they add up quickly. Before long, thick grime collects and thwarts my ability to see clearly. So it is with my inner view of others. One judgment leads to another and another until the tally creates a barrier between us. This cloudiness of thought drifts me away from their positive qualities—my judgments disconnect me from their goodness. So both the other person and I suffer from my lack of mental kindness.

---

Clear-Seeing Friend,
the windows of my mind have smudges
that require daily, attentive cleansing.
Lead me to view others with a kind heart,
to mentally set aside my negative judgments
in order to appreciate their basic goodness.

*Today:* I detect any smudges on my inner window
and clear them off.

# TRUSTING THE HEALING PROCESS

They brought to him a deaf man who had an impediment in his speech; and they begged him to lay his hand on him. [Jesus] took him aside in private, away from the crowd, and put his fingers into his ears, and he spat and touched his tongue. Then looking up to heaven, he sighed and said to him, "Ephphatha," that is, "Be opened."

—Mark 7:32–34

This manner of healing appears rather gross to me. Who would have thought the man would find his hearing and speech recovered in such a way? Amazingly, there is no reluctance or pulling back on the impaired man's part. He willingly submits to how these precious sources of communication are returned to him, no matter how unusual it may have seemed. Oh, for that kind of confidence and vulnerability. I would probably have looked at that spit and said, "Really? Why not just place your hands upon me like you do with other people who come to you?"

I think about my expectations of how the hurts in my life can be mended. Am I truly available to how this could happen, or do I resist the ways that the Holy One enters my mind and heart? What if it's someone I dislike who is to be the instrument for my needed growth, or an experience I resist that is meant to be the source of the peace and inner freedom I've long desired? Am I as open to my transformation as the man whom Jesus healed?

---

Surprising Healer,
when I fail to believe and fully trust
that the kind of inner changes I seek
can be freed from their imprisonment,
remind me that anything is possible
when it comes to how you touch my life.

*Today*: I explore my outlook on ways that I might grow spiritually.

# FAILURE

Then Jesus said to them, "Prophets are not
without honor, except in their hometown, and
among their own kin, and in their own house."
And he could do no deed of power there, except that he laid his hands on a few sick people
and cured them.

—Mark 6:4–5

Jesus did not always prosper at everything he tried to ac-
complish. When Jesus visited his hometown, he discov-
ered how much his ability to teach and heal threatened the
people there. Even though he desired to help, he could do
very little because of their negativity. In this experience,
we join with the humanity of Jesus. It's helpful for us to
be aware of this reality when we have our own defeats.
Not all of our ideas and hopes have the good fortune to
be accomplished. Unexpected and unwanted incidences
of various sorts stall our attempts to move forward with
our abilities and plans. Like Jesus, we discover that a lot

depends on how others respond to our efforts. We may do everything suitably and still something or someone interferes to botch our work.

Jesus did not let his disappointment in Nazareth deter him from continuing to minister to other people in the future. Fortunately, we are also given opportunities to try again, with the assurance that we can learn and grow from what did not turn out as we had hoped. Letdowns are a part of each life. When they happen to us, it's good to remember Jesus had his bummer situations too.

---

Exemplar of Steadfastness,
life does not always unfold as I plan.
When what I have tried does not succeed
and I'm left defeated and disappointed,
turn me toward your own experience
of not achieving what you hoped to do.

*Today*: I deliberately move on from an old failure
that still bothers me.

# SECOND WEEK OF LENT

# GRIEF

> When Jesus arrived, he found that Lazarus had already been in the tomb four days. . . . When Jesus saw [Mary] weeping, and the Jews who came with her also weeping, he was greatly disturbed in spirit and deeply moved. . . . Jesus began to weep.
>
> —John 11:17, 33, 35

While this narrative contains a theological teaching (a prelude to the resurrection of Jesus), it also presents another aspect. This is the story of human grief that slashes the heart and renders it limp with sadness. Jesus weeps for the death of his friend Lazarus and for the loss experienced by Lazarus's sister Mary, whose tears add to his sorrow. This tearful response to a significant loss is common to most everyone at some point. When the COVID-19 pandemic led to the deaths of millions of people across the globe, researchers found that for every deceased person an average of nine people mourned that loss. Grief spares no one.

Many persons I've cherished have died and left an empty, aching place in my heart. If there is one thing I have confidence about, it is that the Holy One hears our cries of lament and gathers us in a tender embrace of love, whether we feel that embrace or not. This may be challenging to believe for someone whose family member is violently killed, a parent embracing a deceased child, a lover kissing the beloved one last time, or someone whose soul friend will never again be there to listen and understand. And yet, that invisible Love never leaves us.

---

Consoler of Those Who Mourn,
even though the death of those I love
shreds my heart into splinters of sorrow,
you do not abandon me to this heartache.
Be with all who stand before coffins today.
Ease their sadness and catch their tears.

*Today*: I lean my losses on the heart of the One
who wept for his friend.

# DISMISSING THOSE WHO SUFFER

> Bartimaeus . . . a blind beggar, was sitting by the roadside. When he heard that it was Jesus of Nazareth, he began to shout out and say, "Jesus, son of David, have mercy on me!" Many sternly ordered him to be quiet. . . . Jesus stood still and said, "Call him here."
>
> —Mark 10:46–49

While I wouldn't think of ordering a person who's had a tough life to keep quiet about their pain as the crowds did to Bartimaeus, I have chosen to make a false excuse and step away from a person hoping to be heard because that person's account of distress would interfere with my planned day. Have you ever nonchalantly asked somebody "How are you?" without intentionally wanting to know? And then have you had your "precious time" absorbed by them actually answering you with considerable length in describing a chronic illness or an unresolved personal difficulty? Or have you tried to avoid an unexpected meeting of certain people who inevitably will go on and on about their unresolved issues whenever you happen to be with them?

These instances are not all that different from the crowd that tried to silence Bartimaeus. They considered him an interference, a nuisance, an interruption to the bigger event that absorbed them. Jesus wouldn't stand for that kind of thing. He stopped. He paid attention. Then his concerned heart led him to reach out with care and restore the man's sight. We may not be able to heal physically, but we can take a break from our plans and schedules and listen kindly to those who hope to have someone pay attention to them.

---

Attentive Healer,
when I prefer to turn away or hide out from
the woes and troubles of those who suffer,
steer me beyond my self-oriented desires.
With your grace, I can gladly reach out
and offer the gift of my listening presence.

*Today*: I listen and am attentive to anyone I encounter.

# OUT OF CONTROL

> Immediately a man out of the tombs with an
> unclean spirit met him. . . . No one could re-
> strain him any more, even with a chain. . . . He
> was always howling and bruising himself with
> stones. When he saw Jesus from a distance, he
> ran and bowed before him; and he shouted at
> the top of his voice.
>
> —Mark 5:2–3, 5–7

Mark's gospel paints a vivid picture of the person referred
to as "the Gerasene demoniac," a man completely beside
himself, unable to control his body or spirit. Was Jesus
initially frightened that this wild figure overtaken with
violent seizures might cause physical harm to him? He
certainly had good reason to be. Imagine the terrifying
scream in the man's voice when he came rushing toward
Jesus, landing at his feet. If Jesus was alarmed, it did not
stop him from extending the tenderness of his empathic
heart. He interacts with the distraught man and then frees

him from the mental and emotional suffering that imprisoned him in his life.

Have you ever found yourself out of control? Yelling at someone when overcome with anger? Unable to stop shaking from shock? Consumed with a gnawing envy, suffocating self-pity, intense withdrawal from others, or another emotional response that chained you to the graveyard of your unrestrained self? More than once I've been able to identify my own internal disturbances with the man Jesus chose to heal. This has helped me to be more compassionate toward others when they are caught in their uncurbed emotions.

---

Source of Serenity,
what amazing kindness you extended
to the man overpowered by his attacks.
When emotional and mental responses
leap around inside of me and defy restraint,
calm me with remembrance of your presence.

*Today*: I seek and find the peaceful regions within
my mind and heart.

# FEAR

When evening came, the boat was out on the sea, and he was alone on the land. When he saw that they were straining at the oars against an adverse wind, he came towards them early in the morning, walking on the sea. . . . They thought it was a ghost and cried out; for they all saw him and were terrified. But immediately he spoke to them and said, "Take heart, it is I; do not be afraid."

—Mark 6:47–50

I recall how scared I felt while canoeing alone on a Minnesota lake. I wasn't very good at rowing, but I felt confident I'd be OK because of the tranquil water when I headed out. A half hour later, a fierce wind came up and I found myself paddling hard, panicked that I'd not make it back to land. With a lot of tough rowing, I finally managed to get the canoe near the shoreline where the water became calmer. I wonder what I would have done had

Jesus come walking toward me on those choppy waves. I understand the disciples' fearful response. Focused on getting their boat back to shore, they weren't looking for divine help walking toward them in that acutely surprising manifestation.

When we come face-to-face with the Holy One's disturbing entrances in their growth-filled arrivals—such as an alarming medical report, a distressing relationship conflict, or anything else that disrupts our normal way of going comfortably about our days—Jesus says to us, as to his disciples, "Take heart, it is I; do not be afraid."

---

Unexpected Visitor,
you come to me during unexpected situations
that erupt and disturb my secure life.
Strengthen my faith in trusting your presence
and my ability to recognize and receive you
in the unpredictable ways you choose to visit me.

*Today*: I hear the Holy One say to me, "It is I; do not be afraid."

# LESS THAN WE HOPED TO BE

> And there was a leper who came to him and knelt before him, saying, "Lord, if you choose, you can make me clean." [Jesus] stretched out his hand and touched him, saying, "I do choose. Be made clean!"
>
> —Matthew 8:2–3

The physical disease of leprosy caused extreme suffering in the time of Jesus. Infected persons were considered untouchable outcasts. This dreaded disease, readily treatable by today's medicines, serves as an image for our approach to the unwanted parts of our personhood—what we consider to be an outcast, something about ourselves that we abhor but cannot flee. This part we detest, whether it is attitude or action, leaves us being less than we could be. This shunned aspect of self is what we confess repeatedly—the familiar lapses that keep showing up in our lives. We make endless efforts to curb anger, to cease disturbing thoughts and feelings, and to forego jealousy or self-pity, yet nothing seems effective.

The story of the leper relates to one of the missing pieces that kept me from being more than I could be. In my early adult years, I became aware of my insistence on being "right" when having a divergent opinion from someone else. After recognizing this defect in myself, I prayed to the Great Healer for spiritual transformation— that I "be made clean" of my interior malady. After some years of making a considerable effort, gradually my attitude altered and "my leprosy" became healed.

How little effort it took for me to ask and how much came from doing so.

---

Healer of Interior Maladies,
I ask to be made clean of whatever
prevents me from being my truest self.
Stretch out the graced hand of your healing;
touch the diseased part of my interior life
and transform what keeps me from being whole.

*Today*: I bring to the Great Healer what requires
changing in myself.

# COMPASSION FATIGUE

A great windstorm arose, and the waves beat into the boat, so that the boat was already being swamped. But he was in the stern, asleep on the cushion.

—Mark 4:37–38

When reflecting on this story, writers and preachers typically tend to focus on the storm, the fearful disciples, and Jesus awakening and calming the tempest. There's another noteworthy detail here: Jesus is apparently exhausted, so much so that he slips into a deep sleep during the thrashing water and wild wind. While some people are sound sleepers and never hear a crashing thunderstorm, it seems more likely that Jesus felt worn out from the constant crowds pressing on him, from the stress of meeting their cries for restoration and reprieve, and from rarely being alone. Add to that cause for weariness: the tiredness of walking from place to place. No public transportation for him. The best he received was a ride in the boat.

Today we would term what Jesus experienced as a type of *compassion fatigue*. This results from daily caregiving without relief. It leads to an eventual depletion of energy that cannot be readily recouped with a few nights of sleep. Medical center staffs on endlessly long shifts, parents continually attentive to drug-addicted children, overworked hospice personnel, first responders during an intensive crisis, social workers with relentless demands, and spouses caring for a partner with Alzheimer's—they understand why Jesus slept during the raging storm. What presses upon you today? Get into the boat with Jesus. Listen to the advice he offers you about what happened to him.

---

Preserver of Inner Peace,
you were there sound asleep on the cushion
while turbulence jolted and terrified others.
When I experience the wild storms of my life,
resurrect in my memory the picture of you
resting and restoring your de-energized self.

*Today*: I permit myself to rest and revitalize my
body and spirit.

# EMBARRASSMENT

On another sabbath he entered the synagogue
and taught, and there was a man there whose
right hand was withered. The scribes and the
Pharisees watched [Jesus] to see whether he
would cure on the sabbath, so that they might
find an accusation against him. Even though
[Jesus] knew what they were thinking, he said
to the man who had the withered hand, "Come
and stand here." He got up and stood there.

—Luke 6:6–8

The surprise of being called forth to stand before a
group could easily produce a feeling of distressing self-
consciousness. Having a disability is not a reason to be
uncomfortable, but onlookers can activate this response
by the way they stare at a person different from themselves. How was it for this man? Was he reluctant to stand
in front of those hypercritical professors?

At a Eucharistic liturgy, I sat near a man with a steel hook for a hand. At least a half dozen times, I stole secret glances at that hand, wondering what happened and how he could manage with it. I imagine much the same for the man with the withered hand—the gawking he received and the cold indifference implied in their stares that led him to want to be anywhere but there. Jesus approached this and other disabilities with an empathic gaze, one that sought to generate relief rather than satisfy callous inquisitiveness. May this be the intention of our hearts when we are with those whose physical features differ from our own.

---

Kind-Eyed Gazer,
your way of seeing led to a sense of well-being;
may I become more aware of the way I look
upon the disparities of other people,
to approach impairment with kindliness
rather than the prying eyes of curiosity.

*Today*: I become more aware of how I view others
who are different from myself.

# THIRD WEEK OF LENT

# LONELINESS

> A Samaritan woman came to draw water, and
> Jesus said to her, "Give me a drink." . . . Then
> the woman left her water jar and went back
> to the city. She said to the people, "Come and
> see a man who told me everything I have ever
> done!"
>
> —John 4:7, 28–29

In *Earth's Wild Music*, Kathleen Dean Moore refers to the
calls of wolf and loon as mournful voices of loneliness.
At the same time she finds beauty and comfort in them:
"the keening of all humankind, all of us together in one
infinite night, all of us floating in the same darkness, each
of us, as we howl our loneliness, finding that we are not
alone after all."[1]

Jesus recognized loneliness when he came upon it.
This time it was the Samaritan woman whose suffering
accompanied her when she walked toward him. He could
sense the hollow spot in her, deep as the well from which

she planned to draw water. Through his patient questions, Jesus led her to see her true value. She slowly believed she had much to receive from his generous kindness and a lot of goodness she could offer to others. As Jesus restored a sense of purpose in this woman lost to herself, she regained her courage and knew she could trust her neighbors to recognize her worthiness. The loneliness that held its sharp blade to her heart was thrust aside. She raced back to encourage them to come and meet the One who convinced her that she was not alone after all.

---

Keen Listener,
you abide patiently by the well of my life,
ready to soothe when loneliness pays a visit.
You wait for me to acknowledge what it is
that sometimes calls out like a howling wolf,
longing to find a home in my deserted self.

*Today*: I communicate with someone who suffers from loneliness.

# HELPFUL, HEALING HANDS

> Now Simon's mother-in-law was in bed with a
> fever, and they told him about her at once. He
> came and took her by the hand and lifted her
> up. Then the fever left her.
>
> —Mark 1:30–31

Have you noticed how often Jesus uses his hands to make
contact when he eases the suffering of someone he encounters? He could just as well have stood at a distance,
so strong was the healing power going forth from him. Instead, Jesus chose to come "up close and personal" when
he met persons who suffered, an indication that he wanted to be near so they felt he was united with them. This
comforting gesture reminds me of St. Teresa of Avila's
oft-quoted saying: "Christ has no body now but yours.
No hands, no feet on earth but yours." With this decla-
ration, Teresa invites us to be "Christ to one another," to
carry on the life-giving gestures of Jesus.

I wonder if parents changing their child's diaper or a teacher cleaning up an ill student's vomit ever consider how their hands are extensions of Christ's own hands. I wonder if any of us think that what we do, whether helping to carry in groceries, folding laundry when it's the other person's duty, shaking hands with an immigrant, writing a note of sympathy, or offering an arm to support someone weakened from age, is similar to that marvelous hand that Jesus gave to Simon's mother-in-law. Gaze upon your hands. How have they eased someone's hurt or helped another in need?[1]

---

Accessible Companion,
you reach out your hand to touch my heart
when I am troubled or feeling out of sorts.
I only need to reach back and receive from you
the attentive care and encouragement you offer.
With my hands and heart, I'll do the same for others.

*Today*: I use my hands to lessen someone's suffering.

# WEEPING FOR WHAT IS TO COME

> As he came near and saw the city, he wept over it, saying, "If you, even you, had only recognized on this day the things that make for peace! But now they are hidden from your eyes."
>
> —Luke 19:41–42

Jesus recognized what lay ahead in the future destruction of the temple in Jerusalem. When he anticipated how this would affect the residents there, this perception summoned deep sorrow for them, so much so that his tears of compassion flowed. No matter how Jesus tried to convince the inhabitants of this future disaster, he knew that his message would be denied or ignored. No wonder he cried.

Foreseeing an oncoming tragedy, or sensing someone's demise, carries its own feeling of ache in that awareness.

There's a chasm of isolating bleakness, knowing that unless a critical change takes place, major harm will result. Many hearts today carry the kind of angst that led Jesus to weep. Climatologists know well the extreme damage to our planet, but their warnings are not believed; grandparents fear a nuclear war in their own or their grandchildren's future; family members' attempts falter in preventing a loved one from catapulting into self-harm; medical staffs observe patients dying who could live had they been vaccinated; marriages fall apart because one partner refuses counseling; and pastors presenting spiritual growth opportunities are ignored by their congregations. Sometimes it is our own self that we weep over, knowing how we need to change for the better but cannot muster what it takes to do so.

What is the "Jerusalem" that you weep over?

---

Far-Seeing One,
your clear vision and hope for the future
fell on deaf ears and failed to make a difference.
When the changes that I long for do not happen,
I will place myself standing alongside your
heart-wrenching tears for what lay ahead.

*Today*: I grieve for the unrest and the conflicts encompassing our world.

# DEPRESSION

His disciples came and took the body [of John the Baptist] and buried it; then they went and told Jesus. Now when Jesus heard this, he withdrew from there in a boat to a deserted place by himself.

—Matthew 14:12–13

Since centuries before our modern era, depression has been named and described in a variety of ways. Modern medicine defines it as an illness causing mood disorders, but Hippocrates, a Greek physician who lived four centuries before Jesus, labeled it "melancholy." Hippocrates identified mourning as a reason for this ongoing sadness. Today we know there are numerous causes for it, but anyone who has been depressed knows how negatively this affects our mental and emotional well-being, with persistent feelings of self-defeat, emptiness, loss of interest, and the ongoing weariness and desire for social isolation. Did Jesus experience depression? It would seem so. Imagine what it was like for him to receive word that his beloved cousin, who passionately supported him and even baptized him in the Jordan, had been murdered. Surely John's cruel death by beheading affected Jesus deeply. No wonder he felt he had to leave and withdraw from everyone.

Unfortunately, depression is a common malady today. Countless people experience a form of this illness, some of it severe enough to require medication or hospitalization. This widespread affliction affects us either through our own hollow feelings and destabilizing thoughts or as we accompany those we know who struggle with this joy-depriving visitor. Let us be patient and loving with ourselves and others when depression takes over.

---

Loving Spirit,
when ongoing depression invades my life
and defeats my ability to feel happiness
about who I am or what I believe I can do,
come to me with your consoling love.
Cradle me in the arms of your compassion.

*Today*: I look intently for snippets of joy in the crevices of my life.

# HYPOCRISY

Do not do as they do, for they do not practice
what they teach.

—Matthew 23:3b

When I was in my early thirties, the pastor in our parish
gave fiery sermons regarding sexual sins. All the while he
preached this to us, he was having an affair with a married woman. He eventually chose to leave the priesthood.
When his reason for doing so became known, the congregation suffered greatly from his hypocrisy. Their trust
in the integrity of a leader fell apart. After that painful
deceit, some families left the parish and never returned.

Hypocrisy causes untold damage either directly or
indirectly. Lying, cheating, thinking one's self better than
others, expecting perfection from someone else while
dismissing personal deficiencies—these are some of the
ways the face of hypocrisy shows itself. We can cause
suffering to others by our haughty expectation that they

should not fail or make mistakes. At the same time, we casually ignore our own faults and failings. For example, I can fume with irritation when another driver does not signal while making a turn at a street corner, but I think nothing of my driving over the speed limit. Or I find myself becoming impatient with those who dilly-dally with their responsibility to carry out programs I've initiated, but I give myself ample excuses for why I've not completed the projects with which I am tasked. "Walking our talk," living with integrity, making sure we comply with what we expect others to observe—these keep us from causing suffering.

---

Encourager of Honesty,
when I am caught in a form of hypocrisy,
guide me to see my lack of integrity.
May I be as forgiving toward others
who do not act in ways that I desire
as I am toward my own faults and failings.

*Today*: I reflect on when and how I "walk my talk."

# MOVED WITH COMPASSION

> I have compassion for the crowd, because they
> have been with me now for three days and have
> nothing to eat. If I send them away hungry to
> their homes, they will faint on the way—and
> some of them have come from a great distance.
> —Mark 8:2–3

The empathic care Jesus expressed for the departing people moves my heart to develop that same spirit of concern. He put himself in their place, recognizing not only
their food insecurity but also their lack of energy to walk
in the hot sun on the long way home. Jesus understood
and was concerned with the consequences of what this
hunger could do to them—the suffering caused by dehy-
dration and sunstroke.

Empathy like that of Jesus requires looking beyond
self to a concern for others. He could gladly have sent the
crowd off, relieved that his three days' work was completed. He must have been exhausted from continually

speaking and mingling with the crowd. Instead, his heart turns toward *their* interest; he imagines what their homeward journey will be like for them. This is the epitome of compassion: alert consideration and then responding to the suffering that one recognizes. A magnanimous spirit bearing boundless love will turn to the other person's hurt and tend to that person's welfare, even if self-compassion also awaits necessary attention. We require and are worthy of self-compassion, but in this case, caring for others came first. Such was the heart of Jesus, and such can be our heart when the situation presents itself.

---

Empathic Heart,
how keen was your heartfelt awareness
of the suffering residing in the lives of others;
how tender was your boundless compassion
in moving beyond your own concerns.
Enhance my empathy so I, too, see and respond.

*Today*: I disregard my troubles long enough to offer support to someone else.

# Poor Self-Image

He entered Jericho and was passing through it. A man was there named Zacchaeus; he was a chief tax collector and was rich. He was trying to see who Jesus was, but on account of the crowd he could not, because he was short in stature. So he ran ahead and climbed a sycamore tree to see him.

—Luke 19:1–10

When Jesus noticed a short man sitting in a tree, did he intuit that this person probably endured teasing due to his size? Being short in stature need not be a physical obstacle, although some do view it that way. Maybe Zacchaeus was bullied in school and disdained in adult life. If so, word would have traveled about this wealthy tax collector compensating for a poor self-image by cheating and defrauding people to ensure his success. Surprisingly, Jesus invites himself to dinner at this man's house. Through his awareness of Zacchaeus's hidden hurt, Jesus opens the way for him to realize his true value and to cease his dishonesty.

None of us enjoys being laughed at, whether due to something about our physical features or our personality. We hurt when we are dismissed by those who think they are superior to us. Place yourself in Zacchaeus's situation today, and have Jesus invite himself to the home of your heart. Listen to him tell you about your positive assets. Then make a resolution to do the same for anyone you may have thought less of because they did not match your ideals.

———————————————

Intuitive Presence,
I desire to approach with respect
those who differ from my stilted notion
of what is an acceptable appearance.
Guide me to see each one's worthiness
and to value them for their true merits.

*Today*: I praise a person for his or her positive qualities.

# FOURTH WEEK OF LENT

# ADMITTING WRONGDOING

> [Jesus] said to him the third time, "Simon son of John, do you love me?" Peter felt hurt because he said to him the third time, "Do you love me?" And he said to him, "Lord, you know everything; you know that I love you."
> —John 21:17

Everyone knows what it is like to have caused hurt to another person, whether the hurt be physical, psychological, or social. We can harm by our words and our actions, or by the lack of words and actions. Sometimes angry verbal attacks or unremitting animosity destroys a person as much as a blow to the head or a knife stab in the heart. I can only imagine how wretched and regretful Peter felt after denying he knew his beloved friend. And to make matters even worse, Peter did so when the enemies of Jesus were out to destroy him.

Our wrongdoings may seem mild in comparison to Peter's, yet that does not lessen our responsibility to admit to wrongdoing and its consequences. When we acknowledge our failures and allow remorse to enter our hearts, we begin the journey of traveling beyond guilt and regret. We bring our disloyal selves into the presence of the Assuring Forgiver. We hear the gracious words of Jesus to Peter after his disciple's hurtful transgression, asking Peter if he loves him. We receive that same penetrating question into our hearts. Our yes to that vital query allows us to move forward into a fresh start.

---

Assuring Forgiver,
when I come to you with my remorse,
you breathe your pardoning love
into my heart, that caused the hurt.
Your lavish absolution inspires me to also forgive
when an offender arrives at the door of my life.

*Today*: I ask forgiveness for a wrongdoing of mine.

# REJECTION

> He came to his hometown and began to teach
> the people in their synagogue, so that they
> were astounded and said, "Where did this man
> get this wisdom and these deeds of power? Is
> not this the carpenter's son? Is not his mother
> called Mary?" . . . And they took offense at him.
> —Matthew 13:54–55, 57

When Jesus entered the synagogue of his birthplace, he
stood before those he knew from his childhood and read
Isaiah 61:1–2, a passage about being anointed to bring
good news to the poor. He then applied that prophecy to
himself. This was more than the people could endure—
who did this nobody think he was? Like Jesus, some
leave their home of origin, only to return and find they
are deemed too different to be accepted because of how
they've changed. Perhaps they are honest about their political principles or sexual identity, have chosen a marriage partner of another race or religion, or have more

tattoos on one arm than the combined tattoos of everyone else there.

My hometown is in the rural Midwest. When I was young and a native citizen of the town returned to visit after becoming educated and successful, I occasionally heard comments such as these to describe them: "Too big for his britches," "Too smart for her own good," "Putting on airs"—the implication being that this person was acting way too important. Those on the home front felt threatened, smaller in stature, uncomfortable, and perhaps even jealous. Like the people of Jesus's hometown, their attitude fueled the social rebuffing of the one who had returned home. Rejection always hurts; all the more so when it comes from people who once extended a warm welcome.

---

Unwavering Supporter,
you have felt the fury of deliberate rejection.
You knew the harshness of being socially spurned
by those who could not accept your individuality.
You are a comfort for anyone who feels set aside
because of their giftedness or unique lifestyle.

*Today*: I acknowledge what causes me to snub or
reject someone.

# EXASPERATION

The Pharisees came and began to argue with [Jesus], asking him for a sign from heaven, to test him. And he sighed deeply in his spirit and said, "Why does this generation ask for a sign? Truly I tell you, no sign will be given to this generation." And he left them, and getting into the boat again, he went across to the other side.

—Mark 8:11–13

Jesus becomes exasperated and refuses to give his questioners any more of his time. He does not let himself get entangled in their hard-hearted arguments. Jesus does not always do this, of course. Sometimes he hangs in there and continues dialoguing with those who disagree or do not understand his teaching. But this time he chooses to depart.

Have you been in situations that evoked the same sort of sigh? Have you said, "No use trying anymore. It's not worth the energy. I give up on this"? It could be frustration with political divisions or medical insurance clerks refusing to listen. We don't have "a boat" to whisk us away from our exasperation with circumstances or people. Instead, we continue living with an irritable family member, remain in a frustrating workplace, and keep engaging with a difficult community. But we can emotionally and mentally pull back our determination to change things. We can accept that what we hope for is seeping away too much of our inner harmony.

What might be leading you to a deep sigh—something you can set aside to find your peace?

---

Discerning Teacher,
you knew when it was appropriate for you
to stop trying to engage in further dialogue.
Guide me to value and use my energy wisely
when I, too, sigh with ongoing frustration.
May I know when to let go of my expectations.

*Today*: I reflect on what may need to be set aside.

# A HEALING TOUCH

[A great multitude of people] had come to hear him and to be healed of their diseases. . . . And all in the crowd were trying to touch him, for power came out from him and healed all of them.

—Luke 6:18–19

Stories of suffering people seeking restored health weave through the gospel narratives. In each scene, Jesus responds to their longings for healing. A remarkable power surged through him as he touched those who wanted their lives to change. What was it like to be there among the crowd, to observe this man with his incredible gift of returning to good health the people with physical ailments and inner tribulations?

It is one thing to express awe and admiration for this facility of Jesus, and quite another to realize that we also can lessen the suffering in another person's life. Our facility comes from the love seeded in us at birth, a love with strength enough to positively affect the pain of others. What a difference our compassionate presence makes as an instrument of healing. The energy flowing from the Spirit of Love in us touches the life of someone else with incredible power. I have known this through kind words spoken when I was deeply distraught, caring arms around me when I mourned the sudden death of my brother, and a felt sense of someone praying for me at the time of an intense transition. Nothing instantly miraculous happened, yet those simple gestures served as precious turning points toward my restored vitality.

---

Source of Healing Energy,
you reach into my suffering with your love
and touch with tenderness what aches inside.
Assure me of my ability to make a difference
for those who long to move beyond their hurts.
Your love within me can have a positive effect.

*Today*: I urge the Love within me to go forth to an individual who is hurting.

# BURDENED

> Come to me, all you that are weary and are carrying heavy burdens, and I will give you rest.
> —Matthew 11:28

Jesus looks at the crowds around him, recognizes weariness in their eyes, and sees in their slumped posture burdens weighing them down in both body and spirit. He knows. He has been weary and burdened more than once. With a heart full of compassion, he reaches out and assures them that he will be there for them, that he desires to ease their weighty afflictions. Jesus speaks these same words to us today, at this very moment, whether the heaviness comes from within us—those burdens we've carried for far too long, such as sorrows, regrets, traumatic memories, resentments, and nonforgiveness—or the burdens coming from outside of us, whether personal events and experiences or concern for those beyond us who bear continual troubles and the sting of life's unfairness.

Burdens are inescapable. They come with the territory of living in a human body and a world that refuses our control of much of what takes place. When Jesus promises rest, he offers solace and hope, reliable support that we can lean on, and relief that we are not alone in what we bear. Take time today to get in touch with what burdens you. Sit down. Breathe slowly. Mentally place in your open hands what presses upon you the most. Give this with trust to the Compassionate One who promises to be your source of peace.

---

Rest for My Burdens,
today I bring to you all that wearies
and weighs heavily upon my daily life.
I rest on your compassionate heart,
confident that you will show me
how to maintain my equanimity.

*Today*: I sit quietly to receive the repose that Jesus
      promised.

# FINDING FAULT

One sabbath he was going through the grain-fields; and as they made their way his disciples began to pluck heads of grain. The Pharisees said to him, "Look, why are they doing what is not lawful on the sabbath?"
—Mark 2:23–24

Certain individuals and groups perpetually found fault with Jesus, regarding either his teachings or what he or his disciples did or did not do about the rules imposed on them by religious authority. In this instance, the disciples were obviously hungry from their journey. Their natural response was to reach out and take some kernels of grain for nourishment. Because they were disciples of Jesus, he was questioned and reproached for this behavior, even though the disciples' actions lacked any significant moral consequence.

Faultfinding comments are easy to dish out but hard to accept when returned in a similar manner. In either case, continual disapproval does more harm than good. For instance, one spouse in a marriage can constantly nit-pick another's shortcomings until the relationship reaches a dead end, parents who criticize but rarely affirm their child's behavior intensify the loss of the youth's self-esteem, pastors who persistently tell the congregation how spiritually unfit they are wonder why pews become more empty on Sunday mornings, teachers who endlessly gripe to students about their laziness notice little change in them, and individuals with self-imposed disparagement find it leads only to further discouragement.

What a changed world we would live in if, for every critical comment, a beneficial word of affirmation was also spoken.

---

Wise Counselor,
guide me to be gentle in my observations.
When I hurry to point out the faults of another,
remind me of the ones that dwell within myself.
Imbue any criticism that I feel necessary to give
with the wisdom and spirit of your loving-kindness.

*Today*: I avoid mental and verbal faultfinding.

# ENDING RELATIONSHIPS

If anyone will not welcome you or listen to
your words, shake off the dust from your feet
as you leave that house or town.

—Matthew 10:14

In biblical times, people shook the dust from their feet
to indicate a final separation from a place or the people
to which they once belonged. This action was a visible
and strong sign of a decisive departure. We know from
Jesus's experience there were circumstances when he left
a group that turned against him. He tells his disciples to
do something similar.

Oh, if only decisions about ending relationships were
as uncomplicated as dusting off our shoes. When is it fit-
ting to separate ourselves from others, to let go and acknowledge that we've exerted sufficient effort and that
we ought to move away from what is harmful and no longer worthy of continuance? There may come a time when

we cannot tolerate being stung mercilessly by someone's insistent berating or by another's stubborn refusal to negotiate. Someone may attempt to annihilate our reputation, deceive with no remorse, or cause us bodily, verbal, or spiritual abuse. When we have made a ceaseless effort to turn around the situation to no avail, it may be time to shake off the dust. This action requires keen discernment, seeking wise counsel, continually taking the issue to prayer, and having the toughest courage, especially when it involves leaving a vowed spouse, parting from a sibling, or walking away from a religion that has brought more harm than good.

---

Understanding Friend,
for anyone who must come to a decision
to shake off the dust from a relationship,
enable them to do this with a clear mind
and a peaceful heart, one that is free
from resentment, guilt, and needling regret.

*Today*: I review my life to see if there's anything
from which I need to walk away.

# Fifth Week of Lent

# ACCEPTING THE DYING PROCESS

> While Jesus was going up to Jerusalem, he took the twelve disciples aside by themselves, and said to them on the way, "See, we are going up to Jerusalem, and the Son of Man will be handed over to the chief priests and scribes, and they will condemn him to death; then they will hand him over to the Gentiles to be mocked and flogged and crucified; and on the third day he will be raised."
>
> —Matthew 20:17–19

Jesus went forth on his final journey to Jerusalem, aware of the suffering awaiting him. How brave his heart as he came to terms with an imminent, dreadful death, one that would terribly distress his disciples. Announcing one's approaching demise to others can be as painful as it is to accept this reality for one's self. In listening to a sorrowful parent with terminal cancer painstakingly reveal this news to her children, I heard the double agony in her voice.

We may not be approaching our physical death, but each of us does have a journey to *our own Jerusalem* that involves dying to old habits or facing some part of our current situation that we have to let go of in order to move on to what lies ahead. Changing stubborn patterns that cling to us requires its own type of courage. Whether death involves a physical ending or changing an unhealthy lifestyle, let us look to Jesus and the many who are brave enough to enter what will eventually proceed to a form of new life.

---

Courageous Journeyer,
you turned your heart toward Jerusalem,
bravely facing what could not be avoided.
I trust your Spirit to grant me the courage
to accept and move toward spiritual growth
and whatever those changes require of me.

*Today*: I acknowledge my Jerusalem and pray for
courage.

# CARRYING THE CROSS

> As they went out, they came upon a man from
> Cyrene named Simon; they compelled this
> man to carry his cross.
>
> —Matthew 27:32

As the weight of the Cross was thrust upon Simon, how
did Jesus feel about this man forced to bear it for him?
What was Simon's response? Surely both were emotionally marked by it. When we walk closely with someone's
pain, we can't help but be affected by doing so. Just yes-
terday I visited a friend whose spouse's health continues
to deteriorate from Parkinson's disease. My friend, once
physically healthy and buoyant, looked alarmingly thin.
Her sallow face reflected the stress of a constant caregiver
and the deepening sadness of knowing death crept closer.
Like Simon, an unavoidable circumstance imposed that
cross upon her. She was carrying it with devoted love

while her spouse was also pained for how his disease marred both of their lives.

Matthew notes that Simon was "compelled," which implies Simon did not carry the Cross willingly but with reluctance. But when he looked back on that occurrence, did Simon eventually see the tremendous privilege and gift of stepping in to bear the Cross of Jesus? Perhaps so. Gratitude usually lies hidden until the hard part of accompanying someone else in their suffering has been completed. Whether forced or voluntarily entering into another's painful experience, some of the weight of that person's exertion can be lifted by our caring presence.

Whose cross are you willing to carry?

---

Cross-Bearer,
thank you for the kindhearted individuals
who have been there in my troubling times,
for how they supported and encouraged me,
thereby lessening the painful load I was bearing.
I will come forward and help others when needed.

*Today*: I notice whose cross is heavy and offer to
    assist with it.

# BETRAYAL

Jesus was troubled in spirit, and declared, "Very truly, I tell you, one of you will betray me."

—John 13:21

Layers of emotion filtered through Jesus on that last evening with his disciples: an immense love for the dedicated friends who accompanied him through the years of ministerial ups and downs, sadness as he realized he was physically departing from them, dread of the terrible death sure to follow in the hours ahead, and now this—one of his own about to divulge his presence to those who sought to kill him, all for a cheap financial reward. This betrayal formed the final blow to his journey of love. Jesus could have responded, "I gave you my heart, my time, my teaching, my care. I trusted you as my disciple. There was nothing I would not have done for you. How could you even think of doing this?" But of course, Jesus did not say this. Instead, he allowed Judas the free will to go forth and do the unthinkable.

Betrayal slices through trustworthy relationships, wounding the heart so mortally that it defies mending. Lack of marriage fidelity, nasty fights within families, refusal to stand by a friend in a financial dispute, rejection after giving fully of one's time to help another, or exclusion following untrue rumors spread by a coworker—these types of duplicity leave lasting scars. When we feel betrayed or deceived, let us sit closely by Jesus, who experienced the sharp-edged suffering prompted by this reprehensible deed.

---

Vessel of Faithful Love,
what profound grief entered your spirit,
knowing you were going to be betrayed
by someone you carried in your heart.
When I am deceived or suffer others' duplicity
I will remember the betrayal you experienced.

*Today*: I make a special effort to be honest in what
I say and do.

# COMFORTING CAREGIVERS

> Then he withdrew from them about a stone's throw, knelt down, and prayed, "Father, if you are willing, remove this cup from me; yet, not my will but yours be done." Then an angel from heaven appeared to him and gave him strength.
>
> —Luke 22:41–43

As a prelude to moving into public life, Jesus spent forty days in the wilderness where he faced daunting temptations and "was famished" from daily fasting. At the conclusion of this purifying retreat, "suddenly angels came and waited on him" (Mt 4:2, 11). Once again, at the close of his public ministry, Jesus is in great need of consolation. As in the wilderness, Jesus receives this solace by ministering angels. These comforting caregivers do not prevent his impending death, but they do provide a strengthening presence for him to make it onto the next step of his concluding journey.

Some situations cannot be avoided, such as cancer and other diseases, physically debilitating accidents, unexpected decisions that greatly alter lives, or the death of a beloved due to suicide. What a gift to find our own ministering angels with us at trials such as these. They have come and wrapped their arms around me when I hurt from a severe loss, listened to my confusion and distress when forced to leave a cherished job, brought food and companionship when I was ill, and sent caring messages in cards and words of encouragement with their phone calls.

Who are your ministering angels? How have you been a comforting caregiver to others?

---

Consoling Caregiver,
you received inner strength to endure
during the time of your severe tribulations.
I, too, have known angels in my distresses
who have brought their kindness and care.
How grateful I am for their loving presence.

*Today*: I recall and give thanks for the ministering angels in my life.

# OUR OWN WORST ENEMY

> Peter said to him, ". . . I will lay down my life
> for you." Jesus answered, "Will you lay down
> your life for me? Very truly, I tell you, before
> the cock crows, you will have denied me three
> times."
>
> —John 13:37–38

There's little doubt that Peter had an immense love for
Jesus. He also had a precocious nature and leaped into
action without thinking. He likewise spoke without real-
izing what his words might demand from him later on.
After his insistent outburst that he would die for Jesus,
Peter ended up doing the opposite by disowning him.
This action caused the disciple agonizing sorrow.

Like Peter, there are countless ways we bring about
our own suffering, whether willingly or not. There's a
saying that sometimes we are "our own worst enemy."
It is ourselves, not others, who generate what distresses
and afflicts us, such as taunting ourselves with whom we

84

wish we could be and are not, wanting to be like others instead of appreciating our own positive qualities, demanding we be and do everything perfectly, stubbornly refusing to let go of old resentments, placing expectations on ourselves or others that balloon way out of proportion, clinging onto harmful relationships, disregarding the helpful counsel of those who care, getting entrenched in false beliefs that brew volatile hostility, wallowing in whining and self-pity, refusing the help of others who offer assistance, and ignoring the benefits of exercise and a healthy diet.

It is never too late to cease being our own worst enemy.

---

Kindhearted Pardoner,
you loved Peter even though he failed you,
just as you continue to love each one of us
no matter how often we initiate our own pain.
Encourage us to make helpful choices that ease
the ways we leap into our self-inflicted misery.

*Today:* I determine how I will reduce the suffering
I put on myself.

# SHAME

When Jesus came to the leader's house and saw the flute players and the crowd making a commotion, he said, "Go away; for the girl is not dead but sleeping." And they laughed at him.

—Matthew 9:23–24

Jesus was made fun of; he was treated like a fool who didn't know what he was doing. The gathered crowd had their fixed views of what they decided was possible. Their minds were like closed doors, tightly shuttered windows, or boxes nailed shut. Out of this mindset, they laughed at Jesus's pronouncement regarding the little girl. Theirs was the kind of laughter that engenders shame. Numerous other times Jesus was taunted, none more painful than hanging naked on the Cross while being scorned: "Those who passed by derided him, shaking their heads and saying, 'You who would destroy the temple and build it in three days, save yourself!'" (Mt 27:39–40).

Who of us has not felt the sting of ridicule? Some persons carry painful memories from their childhood. Adults have their suggestions heartlessly scorned. Passersby jeer at homeless persons. Parents know how it is to be mocked by their teenagers. When we are made to feel humiliated, when we are told we're not good enough for acceptance, or when we're shoved aside because something about us does not fit in, shame easily steps forward. Derisive remarks leave lasting welts on the heart. No one deserves to be shamed, no matter what they say or do.

---

Humiliated One,
gather to your compassionate heart this day
people who have been shamed and scorned.
Lead them to move beyond heartless words
and to believe in their inherent worthiness.
May I never intend to discredit another person.

*Today*: I speak kindly to each person I meet.

# RECOGNIZING THE TRUTH

> Then Jesus said . . . "You will know the truth,
> and the truth will make you free."
>                                                   —John 8:31–32

Jesus speaks about inner freedom to his disciples. When we know ourselves well enough to live from our center of goodness, that truth will liberate us to love as our most authentic self. Do we act out of the truth of our inherent virtues, or do we react in a way that adds to the suffering of self and others? I often find it both challenging and painful to confront what I've managed to avoid. One time this jolt of "truth telling" arrived in my early thirties at a weeklong retreat. I woke up to the reality that I was terribly self-centered. This truth stood before me like a rattlesnake about to strike. At first, I despised myself for being this way. Gradually I turned a corner toward hope, believing that I could change—I did not have to remain so focused on myself. This hard truth became one of my best graces, leading me toward eventually becoming compassionate and other-oriented.

Seeing the truth about ourselves does not always mean uncovering something negative or undesirable. We may have disallowed or been unaware of our virtuous qualities, so that "finding the truth about ourselves" can refer to discovering and claiming the constructive qualities that lie dormant within us. This revelation is what rests at the heart of Macrina Wiederkehr's wonderful prayer: "Help me to believe the truth about myself, no matter how beautiful it is."[1]

---

Bearer of Truth,
guide me to a clearer and fuller perception
of the unknown parts of who I truly am.
I desire to set aside any fear of what I might find.
I will gladly proceed in discovering and claiming
whatever will lead to a closer union with you.

*Today*: I ponder a truth about myself that asks for greater acceptance.

# Sixth Week of Lent
# (Holy Week)

# UNFINISHED WORK

> Then they brought the colt to Jesus and threw their cloaks on it; and he sat on it. Many people spread their cloaks on the road, and others spread leafy branches that they had cut in the fields. Then those who went ahead and those who followed were shouting, "Hosanna! Blessed is the one who comes in the name of the Lord!"
>
> —Mark 11:7–9

How quickly life can take a deadly turn. The triumphant shouts of supporters as Jesus rode through the streets would soon be the shouts of a festering crowd yelling, "Crucify him!" Jesus knew his days were numbered, that his enemies would succeed in capturing him. This would be an end to his ministry and the transformation he envisioned for the people he loved. All this had to be let go as he moved closer to Jerusalem. Jesus would leave this world as a human being with his work of inspiring spiritual transformation and providing healing incomplete. Surely this tough conclusion and dashed hope bled into his consciousness as he moved amid the heralding voices of praise.

A time comes when we face our own moments when we can't do it all or realize it's not going to happen. Plans, goals, and yearnings reside in us, but then unpredicted change comes charging in. We ride our own colt of unfinishedness and face the truth that a part of our dreams or hope for the future has to be relinquished. Our expectations and aspirations fall apart like a crystal goblet crashing to the floor.

---

Releaser of Expectations,
there was much more you could have done
for the people whom you tended with love,
but you could not see this to completion.
Your experience helps me accept the reality
that I also have to leave certain things unfinished.

*Today*: I take note of what I have had to leave undone.

# VIOLENCE

> When they heard this, all in the synagogue were filled with rage. They got up, drove [Jesus] out of the town, and led him to the brow of the hill on which their town was built, so that they might hurl him off the cliff. But he passed through the midst of them and went on his way.
>
> —Luke 4:28–30

Picture the volatility of an outraged mob from a news clip of furious people incited to riot and cause injury. Jesus experienced this when he escaped from the pack's anger. He had to have been aware of the bodily danger he was in. This would not be the last time an angry pack was out to get him. On the hill of Calvary his escape route would be a dead end.

Not everyone in a threatening situation avoids the hostility and resentment of others. Forms of physical and emotional brutality exist everywhere. Daily news reports describe homicide, genocide, and war fatalities. Words, too, are hurled in such a way that they cause grave damage. Silence also fosters violence when it holds power over another by shoving people around psychologically, acting as if they do not exist. Refusing to speak to someone treats that person as an object, not valuable enough to be responded to or given attention. Have you experienced someone's violence? Perhaps you have inflicted this weapon of suffering on someone else. In either case, take time today to visit your memories related to violence while being intent on staying close to the heart of Jesus.

---

Protector of the Wounded,
so many people in the world today
suffer from the violence of others.
I will guard my mouth, mind, and heart
so that I do not inflict pain on anyone
by being knowingly aggressive and hurtful.

*Today*: I consider whether I contribute to violence
in some way.

# STANDING BY THE CROSS

> Meanwhile, standing near the cross of Jesus were his mother, and his mother's sister, Mary the wife of Clopas, and Mary Magdalene.
>
> —John 19:25

If the mother of Jesus could speak to us, I'm confident Mary would tell us that the physical discomfort she felt in her aching back and swollen feet from standing for three hours in the hot sun was nothing compared to the interior pain piercing her soul. After she described how each moan of Jesus shattered her heart, she would assure us that she would much rather have had it be herself who bore that pain of crucifixion than her cherished Son. This beloved mother would remind us that the only "crime" her innocent child committed was having an immense love for humanity and a yearning for them to treat one another with care.

Then Mary, being a kindhearted and supportive woman, would move away from her anguish and ask us to turn our thoughts toward parents today who endure standing by the crosses of their children, parents who long to lessen that suffering but are powerless to do so. After that, she might well hold her arms out wide as a gesture of embracing each person whose heart is breaking because they accompany someone in pain whom they dearly love. Mary would end by urging each of us to be compassionately present with others who suffer and to deliberately send forth the love of her crucified Son to anyone who vigils with someone who is dying.

---

Crucible of Pain,
what terrible agony you endured on the Cross.
Added to that was seeing your mother nearby
bearing in her heart the pain that you experienced.
May I be a compassionate presence to others
when I draw near to their crosses of suffering.

*Today*: I let someone who suffers know that I care
about him or her.

# POWERLESS

Father, if you are willing, remove this cup from me; yet, not my will but yours be done.

—Luke 22:42

How agonizing for Jesus to admit an inability to sidestep his coming Passion and death. In the past, he demonstrated so much strength as he guided his ministry and life. Now he humbly submits and acknowledges that he cannot change this dreadful situation. And so, in the last hours of his physical life, Jesus again enters fully into our human condition. Whether we want to admit it or not, none of us has complete rule over how our lives unfold. We try everything possible to preserve our self-reliance and be in control. We do our utmost to make things turn out the way we want—only to find that at some point we, too, are unable to have our journey evolve in a way that completely satisfies us.

Author Chris Anderson reflects on this reality in *Light When It Comes*. He suggests that powerlessness can be a source of profound personal transformation: "Sooner or later we have to face the suffering and emptiness and apparent randomness of the world and of our powerlessness before it. And until then, we can't be healthy. That's the paradox. Until we admit our need, we can never be happy. And that's what Christ did. He embraced the emptiness so completely and lovingly he transformed it forever. . . . The story of Jesus is the story of the letting go and the giving up we have to do every day of our lives."[1]

---

Vulnerable Leader,
your ability to admit to powerlessness
gives me the courage to acknowledge my own.
When it is time to release what I cannot control,
be at my faltering side. Strengthen my intention
to yield what is impossible for me to change.

*Today*: I unite what I cannot change with the experience of Jesus.

# THE HOUR OF ANGUISH

> Then he came to the disciples and found them
> sleeping; and he said to Peter, "So, could you
> not stay awake with me one hour?"
> —Matthew 26:40

What an excruciating question. In Luke's version of this event, he explains how the disciples were "sleeping because of grief" (Lk 22:45). They couldn't muster the courage to face what was happening. Here was the person they relied on. They benefited from his inner strength day after day, relished his keen leadership, and learned so much from his remarkable insights. Yet Jesus's desperation was just too intense for them. They were stunned by the pain and dread in his voice, so much so that evasion by sleeping overtook them.

I've had to keep my mouth shut on more than one occasion when hearing the reason a son or daughter gave for not being with a seriously ill parent: "I just can't stand to see them suffer." This rationale sounds selfish and ungrateful—maybe it is—but I am not the one to decide that. Moving inside the story of the disciples who could not watch an hour with the teacher they dearly loved—this softens my inner rhetoric about those children. But what a consolation it is to have someone care enough to go beyond self-concern, to be there in our hour of anguish—a time when we feel overwhelmed and long for another person to hold our hand, soften the hardness of the situation, offer comfort and understanding, and ease the ache, if even for just a little while.

---

Suffering Servant,
you longed to have someone watch with you,
to soothe the loneliness and ease the fear
spreading through every pore of your being.
Grant me strength and unselfishness to be there
when others enter their daunting time of trial.

*Today*: I recall with gratitude those who have
watched with me.

*Good Friday*

# FEELING ABANDONED

> And about three o'clock Jesus cried with a loud
> voice . . . "My God, my God, why have you
> forsaken me?"
>
> —Matthew 27:46

Jesus felt left alone and forgotten. He lost all sense of consolation by the very one he had trusted as his Abba—the tender Father he communed with in his night vigils. No wonder his voice pierced the air with that anguished cry saturated with despair. Those words of Jesus declared the ultimate sense of defeat, empty and depleted of hope. In his bleak hours of not only being crucified but also feeling desperately forsaken, Jesus knew the type of pain that threads through anyone in the ragged wasteland known as *the dark night of the soul*—the pain of an awareness of divine presence known to provide desperate relief from the fear of oblivion now being vanquished.

Decades ago, I sat by the bedside of a community member. She was my spiritual mentor, a woman fully committed to daily prayer and union with her Beloved. Sr. Perpetua's physical pain came from bone cancer, but it was her spiritual suffering that startled me. She who had relished such a strong union with the Divine whispered in a frail voice, "I'm unable to pray. Everything is dark. I can't find God. Please pray for me." Her experience led me to open my heart to persons unable to conjure even a whisper of felt faith. If we ourselves have not been ambushed by this sense of being deserted by the Holy One, we can steadfastly support those who have felt such agony.

---

Desolate One,
how fully you lived our human experience,
even to the most utter barrenness of soul.
If my faith in you becomes just a distant memory,
remind me of your forsaken cry from the Cross
and draw me close to your empathetic heart.

*Today*: I remember how I have known the Holy One's steadfast love.

*Holy Saturday*

# GIVING OUR LIFE FOR ANOTHER

No one has greater love than this, to lay down one's life for one's friends.

—John 15:13

Laying down one's life for the sake of love and justice has literally been true for many brave and generous-hearted individuals who died for the cause of other people's welfare. Their giving of life was total and complete. But laying down one's life can also involve something other than the precious, physical giving away. I ask myself, *Who waits for me to contribute what I cherish so that he or she will be positively affected? What part of my life do I most value, and who might be the better for my sharing this?* I consider my own time and personal plans to be at the top of that list. I ask myself, *How willing am I to give away these treasured gifts for the sake of another, and when is it necessary to do so?*

These choices and decisions are not easy ones to make; it is often unclear whether opting for self is the right decision or choosing for others is better. We do need to take care of our own well-being. However, I'm aware of how quickly and mindlessly I slip into preferring self over others. I am greatly influenced by the individualistic and self-oriented culture in which I live. Every day evolves a bit differently than the one before, so that's why I believe in daily discernment. Asking the Spirit for guidance is essential if I am to lay down any part of my life for another.

---

Generous Life Giver,
you unselfishly bequeathed yourself to others
even when this gift resulted in your death.
You unselfishly chose loving over being loved.
Reach into the hesitant part of me and dissolve
any resistance to giving such a generous response.

*Today*: I choose one way I will give of myself now
that Lent has ended.

*Easter Sunday*

# Joy beyond Suffering

When the sabbath was over, Mary Magdalene, and Mary the mother of James, and Salome brought spices, so that they might go and anoint him, and very early on the first day of the week, when the sun had risen, they went to the tomb.

—Mark 16:1–2

Several women hurried in the early dawn to anoint the body of Jesus. As precious as the spices they carried was the devoted love stored in their sorrowful hearts. This tender affection, strong as their grief, moved the women onward toward this compassionate deed. As the women walked to the tomb, they could not have envisioned anything that would soften the pain of the previous days. Had they stayed at home, they would have missed the powerful experience of hope that arrived in the angel's announcement.

The story of these women assures us that our suffering, too, can be transformed. When we go forth to anoint others with our attentive compassion, we find that our wounded hearts have something of value to offer them: empathic understanding and intentional care. If we are willing to look beyond self, to reach out to those who bear life's injuries and sorrows and anoint them with our kindness, we will find our own pain lessened. I've known this in my life and in that of others who've borne the weight of suffering. The joy we receive will be not as earth-shattering as the Resurrection of Jesus but more like a slow-flowing stream that gradually washes the pain from our hearts and turns us toward gladness.

---

Joy of My Life,
may the love that dwells within my heart
be as fervent as that of the dedicated women
who intended to anoint your entombed body.
Come and surprise me with the gift of renewed hope.
Revive what has been lying dormant in my spirit.

*Today*: I anoint people around me with the joy of
gladness.

The human spirit is astounding in its resiliency
and its ability to recover hope.
That is what the Resurrection proclaims:
the possibility of transformation,
the belief that we can be filled with new life,
that the future will bless us.
There is new country waiting for us.
There are new melodies that yearn
to be sung in our spirits.
We must believe this even
on our most desolate of days.
The season of springtime, of hello,
awaits us all.

—Joyce Rupp, *Praying Our Goodbyes*

*Questions for Reflection*

---

# FOR PERSONAL REFLECTION AND GROUP FAITH SHARING

Begin by choosing one of the prayers from the week. Pray it aloud. Follow this with a few minutes of quiet time to recall the past week of prayer with *Jesus, Companion in My Suffering*. Then, proceed with the following questions and any other questions or insights you deem suitable for the faith-sharing conversation or your personal reflection.

As you look back over the past week, consider these questions:

1. Which of the reflections most inspired and encouraged you? Did any depiction of Jesus's suffering surprise you or lead you to a new awareness?

2. Have you experienced one of the sufferings from this week? If so, what was this like for you? Who or what helped you to get through it?

3. Which day felt most difficult for you to pray? What made it challenging? Which day did you especially appreciate?

4. Of the sufferings presented this week, which do you find easiest to offer compassion for another person? Which suffering is the toughest for you to extend compassion?

5. If you were to choose an image or symbol to describe the past week of praying with the topics of suffering, what would you choose, and why?

6. How would you describe your Lenten journey thus far?

7. Is there anything else about the reflections that you would add?

Close each time of reflection by praying aloud one of the other prayers from the week.

For the final time of reflection during or after Holy Week, choose a time of quiet to respond to this question: How would you summarize your experience of praying with *Jesus, Companion in My Suffering*?

# Notes

## Introduction

1. Lucy Hone, "The Three Secrets of Resilient People," TED Talk, https://www.youtube.com/watch?v=NWH8N-BvhAw.

2. Marilyn McEntyre, "Our Litanies of Lament," *Give Us This Day*, March 2021, 159–60.

3. Joseph Cardinal Bernardin, "The Gift of Peace," *Give Us This Day*, March 2021, 234–35.

## Saturday After Ash Wednesday

1. Mark Nepo, *The Book of Soul: 52 Paths to Living What Matters* (New York: St. Martin's Press, 2020), 5.

## Third Sunday of Lent

1. Kathleen Dean Moore, *Earth's Wild Music: Celebrating and Defending the Songs of the Natural World* (Berkeley, CA: Counterpoint Press, 2021), 26.

## Monday of the Third Week of Lent

1. Joyce Rupp, "The Hands of Christ," adapted from her reflection in *Living Faith*, January 12, 2022, https://www.livingfaith.com.

## Saturday of the Fifth Week of Lent

1. Macrina Wiederkehr, *Seven Sacred Pauses: Living Mindfully through the Hours of the Day* (Notre Dame, IN: Sorin Books, 2008), 178.

## Wednesday of Holy Week

1. Chris Anderson, *Light When It Comes: Trusting Joy, Facing Darkness, and Seeing God in Everything* (Grand Rapids, MI: Eerdmans, 2016), 247.

JOYCE RUPP is well known for her work as a writer and spiritual midwife. She serves as a consultant for the Boundless Compassion program. Rupp is the author of numerous bestselling books, including *Praying Our Goodbyes*, *Open the Door*, *Return to the Root*, and *Jesus, Friend of My Soul*. Her 2018 book, *Boundless Compassion*, won awards from the Association of Catholic Publishers and the Catholic Media Association. Her books *Fly While You Still Have Wings* and *Anchors for the Soul* also have earned CMA awards. She is a member of the Servite (Servants of Mary) community.

joycerupp.com

# MORE BOOKS BY
## Joyce Rupp